EASY
APPLIQUÉ
BLOCKS

EASY APPLIQUÉ

BLOCKS

50 Designs in 5 Sizes

KAY MACKENZIE

Martingale®
& COMPANY

Easy Appliqué Blocks: 50 Designs in 5 Sizes
© 2009 by Kay Mackenzie

That Patchwork Place® is an imprint of Martingale & Company®.

Martingale & Company
20205 144th Ave. NE
Woodinville, WA 98072-8478 USA
www.martingale-pub.com

Credits

President & CEO ~ Tom Wierzbicki
Editorial Director ~ Mary V. Green
Managing Editor ~ Tina Cook
Developmental Editor ~ Karen Costello Soltys
Technical Editor ~ Robin Strobel
Copy Editor ~ Durby Peterson
Design Director ~ Stan Green
Production Manager ~ Regina Girard
Cover & Text Designer ~ Stan Green
Illustrators ~ Kay Mackenzie & Adrienne Smitke
CD Designer ~ Adrienne Smitke
Photographer ~ Brent Kane

Printed in China
14 13 12 11 10 09   8 7 6 5 4 3 2 1

Library of Congress Cataloging-in-Publication Data
Library of Congress Control Number: 2008045634

ISBN: 978-1-56477-885-7

Mission Statement

Dedicated to providing quality products and service
to inspire creativity.

Acknowledgments

First I give hugs to my husband, Dana Mackenzie, for his steadfast support of all my endeavors, and especially for supporting my desire to no longer have a day job so that I could put all my energy into quilting, writing, and designing. In addition to that, Dana cheerfully eats whatever's put in front of him and then washes the dishes.

Scritches and cheese biscuits go to my little dog, Willie, for his treasured dog help and boon companionship in the studio.

So much gratitude goes to Martingale & Company for taking on my designs and believing in the concept for this book. From the bottom of a writerly quilter's heart, thank you for what is no less than a major life goal for me. Special thanks to Robin Strobel, who led me through this with much patience and humor.

To all the friends, old and brand new, who have given me encouragement and validation—there are so many—thank you for being there with me in our wonderful community of quilting.

Kay

CONTENTS

GREETINGS, FELLOW APPLIQUÉ ENTHUSIASTS!

Gentle quilter, if you're reading this, you're already an appliqué fan. Three cheers! Whether you enjoy the soothing rhythms of hand work or the flying needle of the machine, there's something satisfying about appliqué, both to the quiltmaker and to the viewer. Everyone appreciates the beauty of appliqué, whether they practice it or not. It just seems to bring forth oohs and ahs from the heart.

I felt that pull right away, and I've been an avid appliquér ever since I became a quilter. Over the past few years I found myself creating and stitching designs that included more and more fine detail. One day I designed a simple block with just a few pieces—and it was a breath of fresh air!

I enjoyed the style so much that I set out to create this whole collection of blocks designed with easy sewing in mind. You'll find flowers, baskets, birds, animals, fruits, teapots, hearts, and a whole variety of what can only be described as offbeat and unique designs. Consider this an eclectic library of fun designs that you can reach for anytime you want a block—or many!

The Methods

There are quite a few ways to appliqué, and many variations within broad categories of techniques. Appliquérs sometimes prefer to stick with what they've learned first. Others gravitate toward a certain method that works for them and gives satisfying results. What works is not the same for everybody, and all methods are good! This little book provides designs for your appliqué pleasure using your favorite methods and your own creative instincts.

Beginning on page 31 you'll find information on both hand- and machine-appliqué methods. First there are some general tips, then two preparation methods for traditional hand appliqué. We'll go over what I have to share about hand stitching smooth curves, pointy points, and sharp notches. Following the section on hand appliqué, there's an overview of raw-edge machine appliqué using paper-backed fusible web. Whatever your method, pick your favorite designs and stitch them with fun!

Printing Blocks from the CD

How to Use the CD

From the companion CD located on the back inside cover, you'll be able to print the blocks you've chosen in five different sizes: 6", 8", 9", 10", or 12". Larger sizes will automatically print out as multiple pages; just trim and tape them together and you'll be ready to go! Plus, you can print a reversed version for those appliqué methods that require them. Your life just got easier! No flipping and tracing, figuring of percentages, or trips to the copy shop.

What You Need

The CD is designed to work on PC, Mac, and Linux platforms with the following operating systems:

◆ Windows 2000, XP, and Vista+

◆ Mac OS X 10.3+

◆ Linux (Kernel 2.4+)

To use the CD you need a CD-ROM drive, a PDF reader, and an internet browser. (The browser is what runs the CD and allows you to access any of the links included.) You probably have both pieces of software on your computer already, but if you have trouble using the CD, you may need to upgrade your software.

If you're connected to the internet, you already have a browser. The browser runs the CD whether you are online or not. Some of the really old browsers may have difficulty running the CD. Internet Explorer version 6 and later, Safari version 3 and later, and Firefox version 2 and later all are compatible. You can upgrade your browser by visiting the provider's website.

The actual patterns are PDF files. Examples of PDF readers are Adobe Reader and Mac's Preview. If you don't have a PDF reader installed, you can download Adobe's version for free. Just go to: http://www.adobe.com and download and install the reader that is compatible with your operating system.

How it Works

Insert the CD into your CD-ROM drive. Open the CD and click the *Easy Appliqué Blocks* file to open it. Some browsers may display a warning screen about active content. There is no active content on the CD and you can feel safe about ignoring the warning.

ENTER

Begin by reviewing the copyright information. These are patterns for your own personal use as the owner of *Easy Appliqué Blocks*. It's important to realize that the patterns in electronic form are covered by the same protections as paper patterns. That means, gentle quilter, no printing for a friend, no emailing, no posting on the internet, etc.

The first time you use the CD, it's a good idea to test your printer settings to make sure the blocks are printing at the correct size. Use the navigation bar at the top of the page or the link lower on the page to go to the "Pattern Test" page.

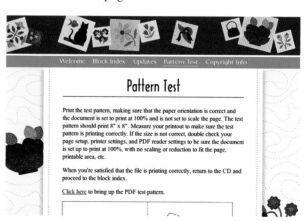

Follow the directions on the "Pattern Test" page to print the test pattern. Some computers think they are being helpful by slightly scaling down files before printing, just to be certain nothing gets cut off by your printer's margin. Unfortunately, there are several places this sizing-down can occur. If the size of the test pattern is not correct, check your page setup, printer settings, and PDF-reader settings to be certain the documents are set to *print at 100% with no scaling or reduction to fit the page, margins, printable area, etc.*

When you are satisfied that the file is printing correctly, return to the CD and proceed to the block index.

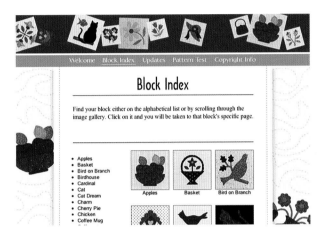

You'll find both an alphabetical list and thumbnail pictures of the blocks. Click on your selected block on either list and you'll be taken to its block page.

On the block page, determine the correct pattern orientation. Freezer-paper-on-top hand appliqué uses regular patterns. Back-basting hand appliqué and fusible machine appliqué use reversed patterns.

Choose your size. Under the correct orientation, click the finished block size you've chosen. The PDF pattern will open. Print your pattern. If the block is larger than will fit on letter-size paper, multiple pages will automatically print. Simply trim and tape them together for your full-sized pattern.

Easy peasy! Once your block has printed, return to the block page. From there you can click back to the "Block Index" and print some more blocks!

The above information also appears on the "Welcome" page so it'll be handy when you're using the CD. When you're done printing, simply eject the CD at any point. Be sure to put it back in its pocket with the book.

Enlarging Blocks by Photocopying

If you don't have access to a computer and printer, you can enlarge the printed designs in the book using a photocopier. The patterns in the book are printed 3" x 3". To enlarge the printed patterns, photocopy according to the following percentages:

6" block—200%
8" block—266%
9" block—300%

For larger sizes, fold the pattern in halves or quarters, enlarge each section to the same percentage, and then trim and tape the sections together.

10" block—333%
12" block—400%

BLOCK LIBRARY

Use these designs wherever your imagination leads you:
wall quilts • aprons • small quilts • sampler quilts • vests • bed quilts •
baby quilts • table runners • lap quilts • nap quilts • banners •
table toppers • totes • thank-you blocks • tea cozies • tea towels •
pot holders • purses • postcards • place mats • jackets •
jumpers • sweatshirts • skirts • mantel covers • dresser runners •
scarves • embroidery patterns

Apples

Basket

Bird on
Branch

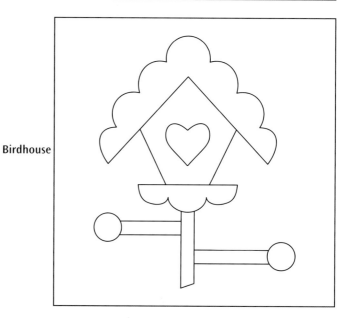

Birdhouse

Cardinal

Cat

Cat
Dream

Charm

Cherry
Pie

Chicken

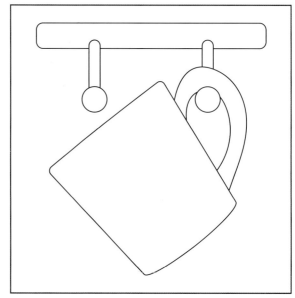

Coffee
Mug

Coffeepot

Crossed
Fleurs

Crossed
Tulips

Daisy

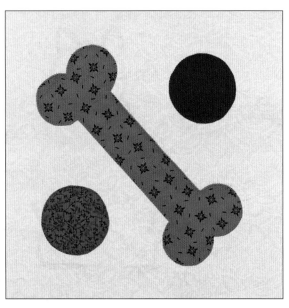

Dog
Bone

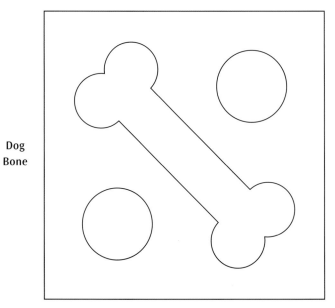

Doves

Flower
Basket

Folk
Heart

Framed
Flower

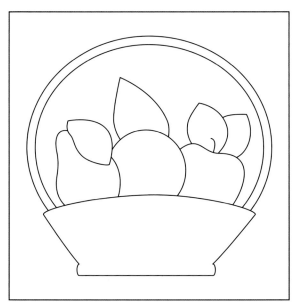

Fruit
Basket

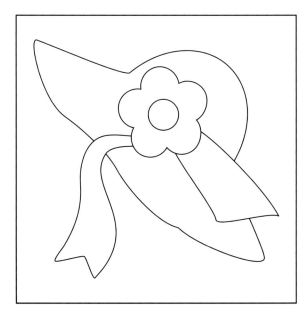

Hat

Heart
and Buds

Heart
Planter

King
and
Queen

Lemon
Flowers

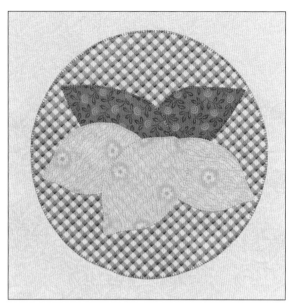

Lemons

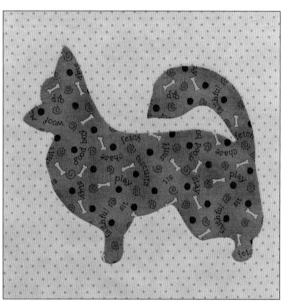

Little Dog

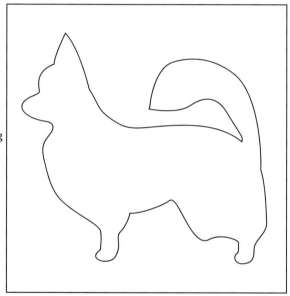

Love

Moon
and Stars

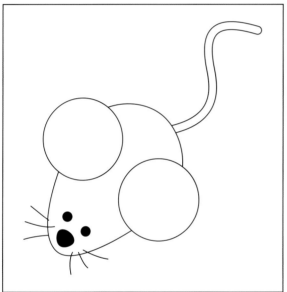

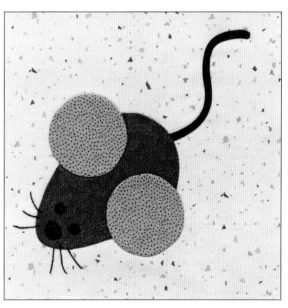

Mouse

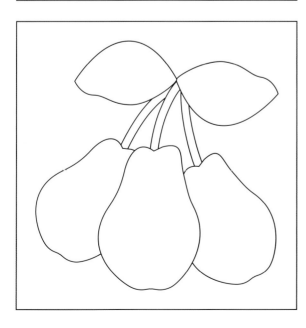

Pears

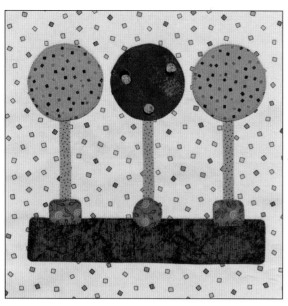

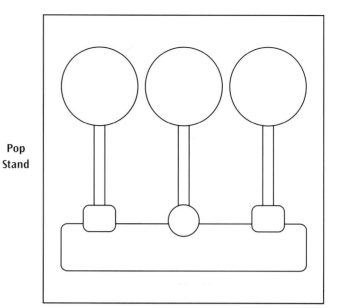

Pop
Stand

Posy
Bunch

Primroses

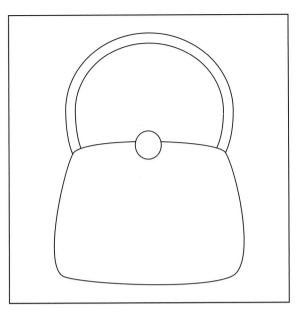

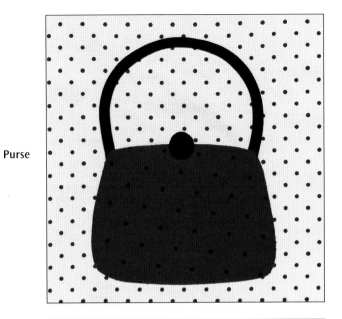

Purse

Rose

Rotary
Cutter

Scottie

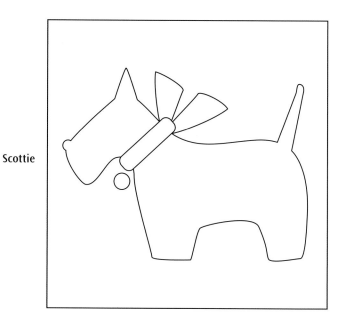

Sit
and Sip

Starflower
and Buds

Sunflowers

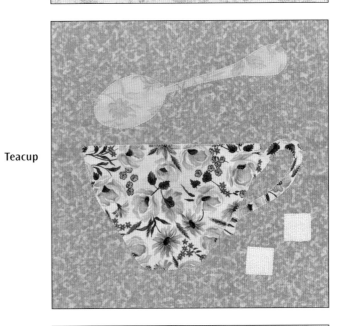

Teacup

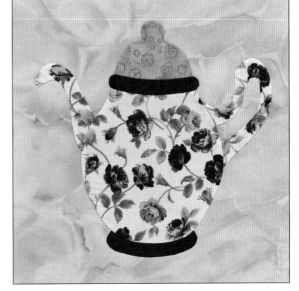

Teapot

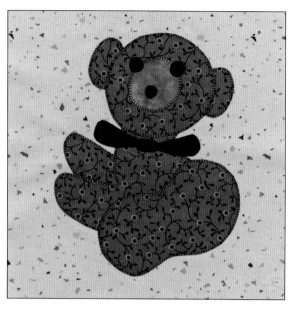

Teddy Bear

Tree

Tulip Trio

Vase

Welcome

Wreath

KAY'S HAND-APPLIQUÉ TIPS

Before we get to the stitching, let's start with some basics.

Vision

If you wear glasses, making sure that your prescription is up-to-date is very important for good appliqué results.

I never needed glasses, but at a certain age I had to admit that I found myself with vision "issues." Does the following sound at all familiar? You can't see the grain of the fabric; you can't find the eye of the needle; you're holding your quilting magazine at arm's length.

Gentle quilter, it's time to go to the drugstore and get some of those groovy granny glasses. Pick up a pill bottle and try on pairs of reading glasses until you can read the teeny, tiny writing on the bottle.

Presbyopia, otherwise known as "over-40 eyes," is a natural process that causes stiffening in the eye's focusing mechanism, making it difficult to see small things close up. Nonprescription reading glasses magnify the small things and add details back to your vision that you may not have noticed were missing for awhile. This is important for good appliqué results.

Lighting

Good lighting goes hand in hand with good vision for supporting the success of your appliqué efforts. If your sewing light is just adequate, make a special effort to arrange for more lighting or lighting that is better directed on your work. Overhead lighting, such as a ceiling light, isn't really sufficient for close-up work. Invest in a lamp for your work area that can be redirected as needed to illuminate your appliqué.

Fabric Selection

Choose 100%-cotton, medium-weight fabric with a soft, pliable hand. Fabrics containing polyester have "spring" and will resist the creasing needed for turning the margin. Too thin or loosely woven fabrics will ravel easily and wear out more quickly. Fabrics found in independent quilt shops are generally of the highest quality and easiest to work with.

A quick word to the wise: prints hide stitches better than solid fabrics. If you'd like to achieve the overall look of solid colors, you can use tone-on-tone prints for added depth and glow. That said, if you're happy with your hand stitching, don't hesitate to use solids if they give you the look you're after.

Fabric Preparation

Some quilters prewash their fabrics to remove the sizing, and some prefer to leave the sizing in for added body when piecing. As an appliquér, I don't care for the sizing. I like the feel of soft clean fabric, so I'm a washer. I don't think the appliqué police will come after you if you're not—just make sure to test any suspect fabrics for bleeding issues.

Tools and Notions

"The right tool for the right job" is an adage that certainly applies to appliqué. Making good selections in the threads, needles, and scissors you use can make a big difference and can help you avoid frustration and achieve results that please you.

Scissors

Use sharp, pointy hand scissors, not big shears. My favorite size is 5"; some quilters use smaller embroidery scissors. These small scissors give you the control you'll need for precise trimming and clipping.

Thread

Use fine, thin thread that matches the piece being appliquéd (not the background). I use 50-weight, cotton, two-ply machine-embroidery thread. Others use 50-weight three-ply or 60-weight thread, and still others swear by very fine silk thread. All of these are good choices for hand appliqué. Use what you can find conveniently.

Needles

Use appliqué needles. Yes, even if you have trouble threading them. Size 10 or 11 straw or milliner's needles (they're the same thing) or size 10 or 11 Sharps are excellent choices. Milliner's needles are longer than Sharps, and many appliquérs feel they can get a better grip on them. My favorite is a size 10 milliner's, because I bend size 11!

Whatever the brand or number, the important thing is that it's a slender needle that glides through fabric easily without resistance.

A Threading Tip

Instead of holding the needle in midair and trying to poke the thread though the eye, try this method. Cut a fresh end of the thread. Pinch the end between your thumb and forefinger. Slowly open up the tips of your thumb and forefinger until the end of the thread is just visible. With the other hand, bring the eye of the needle down over the thread.

Many who swear they cannot thread a needle succeed on the very first try when shown this strategy

Suggestions for Fine Details

There aren't many fine details in these simple blocks, but for the occasional stem, whisker, or eye, you can use a couple strands of embroidery thread, a fabric pen, buttons, or beads.

To embroider a French knot for eyes, bring the needle up from the back of the fabric. Hold the floss taut, wrap it two or three times around the needle, and insert the needle close to where it came up. Pull the thread through to the back.

A stem or outline stitch can be used for the whiskers on the mouse or the stems on the cherries. Bring the needle up from the back. Insert it into the background about ⅜" from the start and take a small stitch at 3, coming up halfway between 1 and 2.

FREEZER-PAPER-ON-TOP PREPARATION

The freezer-paper templates in this classic method help you cut the shapes accurately.
And, if you leave the templates on while sewing, they can define the stitching edge.

Notions

- Freezer paper
- Tracing paper
- Basting needle (an old needle is good for this)
- Basting thread (something you'd like to use up)
- An appliqué needle; use your favorite. (See the information on page 33.)
- Appliqué thread; use your favorite. (See the information on page 32.)
- Sharp, pointy hand scissors
- Light box or light-colored surface
- ¼" or ⅜" bias-tape maker (optional)
- Paper-backed fusible web on a roll (optional)
- Fabric-marking pencil (optional)

Pattern Preparation

This method uses freezer-paper templates ironed to the right side of the fabric to achieve the appliqué shapes. Your finished appliqué will be oriented in the same direction as the pattern.

Select and print a regular pattern from the CD. Larger patterns will print on several pages. Trim and tape the pages together to make the full-sized design.

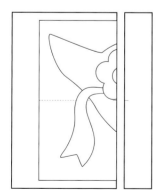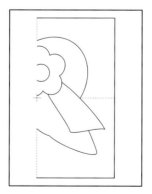

The 10" Hat block prints on two pages. Trim one side of the overlap and tape the two pieces together.

Study the pattern to decide the stitching order of the pieces (aka motifs). Begin with pieces that are partially behind other pieces and build to the front. It's helpful to number the pieces in sequence on the pattern. You can also make note of the fabric or color you've assigned.

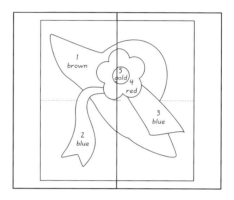

Placement Guide

I use a tracing-paper overlay as a placement guide. To create the overlay, trace the entire pattern onto tracing paper. A pencil is fine for this. Also transfer the horizontal and vertical centering lines that are given on each pattern. You won't need the motif numbers or the color notes on the overlay.

Larger sizes of tracing paper are available at stationery or art-supply stores. Or, you can tape together sheets of tracing paper for larger patterns.

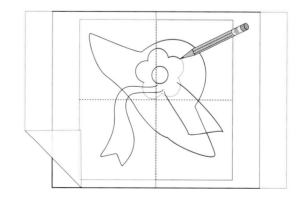

Trace pattern to make a placement guide.

Template Preparation

For motifs other than stems or vines, you'll use regular supermarket freezer paper to make the templates. In this method, the pattern does not need to be reversed. What you see is what you get. From the original pattern, trace each appliqué piece individually on the paper side of the freezer paper. To denote a portion of a piece that is overlapped by another piece, use a dashed line. Transfer the numbers and color notes as well.

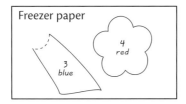

For multiples of the same shape, like leaves, I make a separate template for each piece. Some quilters layer the freezer paper and cut multiple templates at once, but I find more accuracy in tracing and cutting each one individually.

Cut out each template on the drawn line. Where there's a dashed line, cut slightly to the outside of it (so you can see that it's a dashed line).

Scissors for Paper

Many quilters prefer to use a separate pair of scissors for cutting paper, because they feel that paper will dull their good sewing scissors. Don't tell the appliqué police, but I use whatever scissors I can find!

Background-Fabric Preparation

Cut the background square a little larger than the unfinished size. For an 8" block (8½" unfinished), cut the background at least 9" square. After the block is completed, you'll trim it to the unfinished size.

To create positioning marks on the fabric, fold the background square in quarters and crease the outer edges. (You can also add small pencil marks in the creases at the edges of the right side of the fabric—these will be trimmed away later.) On the right side, trace each stem, strip, or vine with one central line, plus a beginning and ending mark. A light pencil mark will suffice for this. No further marking is needed at this point. For example, for this pattern, mark the background square as shown.

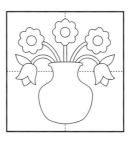 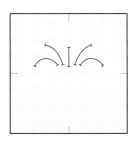

Dark Background Fabrics

When using dark fabrics for the background, it may not be possible to see through the fabric for tracing. In this case, you can use tailor's wax-free tracing paper and a tracing wheel or stylus to transfer the markings.

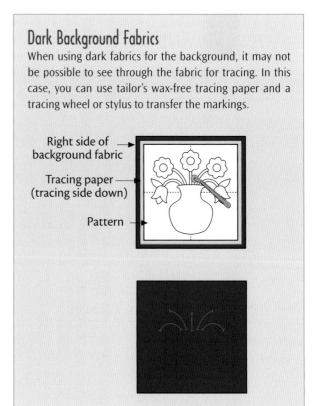

Stems or Vines

When I'm using this method of appliqué and the pattern calls for stems or vines, I reach for my trusty gadget—the ¼" or ⅜" bias-tape maker. This tool automatically folds the edges of the fabric to make bias tape of a nice even width. Bias-tape makers come in progressively wider widths. Just be aware that the wider the bias strip, the less likely it is to go around a tight curve smoothly, without puckering. For wider stems or vines, consider using freezer-paper templates just like other motifs.

Here's how I get the bias-tape maker to work easily for me.

1. For the ¼"-wide gadget, cut a ⅝"-wide strip of fabric on the bias. For the ⅜"-wide gadget, cut the bias strip ⅞" wide. Trim the top of the strip at an angle upward to the left (it seems to feed through the gadget better this way). For straight strips, cut the strips on the straight grain instead of on the bias. They wiggle less.

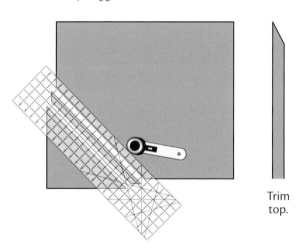

Trim top.

2. Poke the point at the end of strip right side up into the wider end of the gadget until you can see the fabric in the slot on top. Use the tip of a pin to pull the strip along the slot until it sticks out at the narrow end. Pin this folded end of the strip to the ironing board. Be sure to use a glass-head pin so you don't have to worry about melting a plastic pin.

3. Using a hot iron and plenty of steam, pull the gadget along the strip with one smooth, fairly rapid motion, following it closely with the iron. *Hold your iron so that the steam vents are not directed at your fingers.* Don't stop partway through or try to back

up. Pulling smoothly is important for getting nicely formed bias tape.

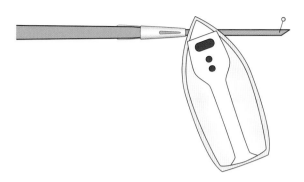

Making Bias Strips Fusible

Instead of basting stems to the background, you can make bias or straight strips fusible by applying thin strips of paper-backed fusible web. The product comes on a roll and can be found alongside the bias-tape makers in the notions section of your favorite quilt shop.

I apply the fusible web with a dry iron as a separate step, right after making the bias tape. I prefer to cut the web in half lengthwise so that there is only a tiny amount applied in the center on the wrong side of the bias tape. This will be enough to keep the stems or vines secure for stitching.

Motif Preparation

1. With a dry iron, not overly hot, press the freezer-paper templates shiny side down onto the *right* side of the motif fabrics, leaving at least ½" between templates. Press just long enough for the freezer paper to adhere. A piece of cardboard underneath the fabric helps create a better bond.

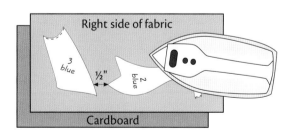

Right side of fabric

½"

Cardboard

2. Allow fabric and templates to cool briefly. Handling them as little as possible, cut the motif area away from the main body of the fabric. Roughly cut the motifs apart, leaving at least ¼" all around.

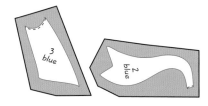

Cut motifs apart, leaving at least ¼" margins.

3. Carefully trim each motif in preparation for appliquéing. A ¼" turning allowance is actually too much for most appliqué pieces. This amount creates bulk and encourages bumps and blunt-ended points. Leave only about ³⁄₁₆, or as little as ⅛" for very small pieces. This makes some quilters nervous, but fine work is achieved through this closer trim.

   Leave a little bit wider turning allowance on any edge that will be overlapped by another piece, as indicated by a dashed line on the template.

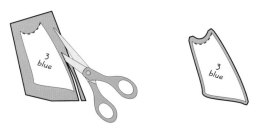

Protect Your Appliqués
Keep your motifs in a little box or a file folder. Leave the templates on and handle them as little as possible until ready to sew.

Decision Time

This is the point at which you'll decide whether to leave the freezer paper on while sewing or take it off.

Removing the templates means you'll be stitching in traditional hand appliqué mode, with no marked line to follow. You'll develop an appliquér's sense of the right amount to turn under. This is very pleasant stitching, my favorite way to work. However, I do sometimes leave the freezer paper on when I feel the need for extra control over placement and shape.

If you prefer appliquéing with a marked line, you can use a fabric-marking pencil to trace around the templates on the right side of the fabric before removing them. Be sure to turn the marked line all the way under when stitching so that it will not be seen.

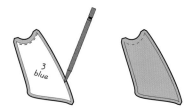

Stitching with the freezer paper on facilitates precise, flat work. The edge of the paper provides a crisp, identifiable turning line. The stitching technique is the same, though you'll need to tip the sewing edge up toward you slightly to avoid catching the paper. In some instances the paper actually gets in the way. When this happens, you can fold a portion of the paper back, stitch the area, and then replace the paper. I often stitch star points this way. You can also tear away a section of the template or remove the whole thing partway through if you no longer need it. Remember, the template is there to help you, not hinder you.

Positioning Motifs

Putting the pieces where they're supposed to go is easy and accurate using a combination of direct marking for stems and the placement guide for everything else.

Stems, Vines, and Straight Strips
These elements are usually the first ones to be stitched—we sew as plants grow. Position the prepared strips along the previously marked lines on the background fabric (see "Background-Fabric Preparation" on page 36). Be sure to leave a generous extra length at each end of the strips. You can easily trim off what you don't need later.

If you've applied fusible web along the back of the strips, remove the paper backing and fuse them in place with a hot steam iron, molding the strips along curves.

If you haven't used fusible web, there are a couple of other ways to hold the strips in place for stitching. I've found that a little glue can be my friend. A dab of glue stick works fine to secure these elements in place for stitching. Or, you can thread baste them in place.

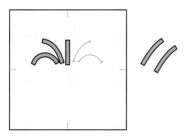

Other Motifs

Place the motif on the background near where you think it might go. Lay the placement guide on top and align the center marks on all four sides with the marks or creases on the background. Without shifting the placement guide, reach underneath and nudge the motif into place.

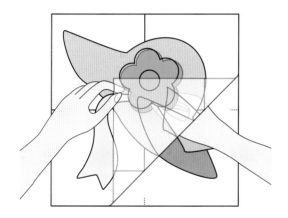

If the template is on the motif, it will line up exactly with the traced shape. If the template has been removed, adjust the motif until an equal amount of the turning allowance is visible all the way around the outside of the traced shape. (An extra amount of fabric margin will be visible in areas that will be overlapped.)

Lay the guide back down, recheck the centering marks, and recheck the motif placement. When all is satisfactory, remove the guide, and without shifting the piece, baste it in place. You can baste right through freezer paper.

Securing Motifs

Many accomplished appliqué artists pin their motifs in place for stitching. I achieve more satisfactory results by basting with needle and thread. It only takes a few seconds to baste each piece, there are no pins to contend with, and the interior of the motif lies flat. You can use an old needle and any type of thread for basting.

Baste fairly close to all stitching edges, leaving enough room to turn the margins under. When the project is folded or rolled so you can get a proper grip on it, the edges of the motif will not be able to shift.

Now you're all prepped and ready to start stitching! My tips for smooth curves, sharp notches, and pointy points continue on page 45.

A Piece at a Time

I feel that it's best to position and sew one motif at a time to minimize handling. The more the motifs are handled, the more potential for frayed edges and loosened freezer paper.

Back-Basting Preparation

If you like hand appliqué, you might just love this preparation method. It's not new, but it may have been flying under the radar for a lot of appliqué fans.

I heard about back-basting—aka the no-template method, aka the template-free method—a number of times before I finally wrapped my brain around it. Once I tried it, I was quickly convinced of its benefits.

Whatever you call this method, there's no faster way to get to the stitching. Cut a background square, select your appliqué fabrics, trace the pattern once, and sew!

Compared to using templates, this technique eliminates several steps in preparation and placement. Plus, the pieces can't shift out of place and are very accurately sewn.

The preparation is very different in this method, but the actual stitching of the motifs is just the same as in traditional hand appliqué. Stitching order is also the same—start with pieces that are partially behind other pieces and build to the front. Clipping of curves and notches is just the same. Points and notches are also stitched the same way.

Once you see how it works, put back-basting into your appliqué bag of tricks and use it whenever you like. Start with projects that have bigger pieces and work your way to smaller ones as you become more comfortable with the method.

Overview

With this method, your finished appliqué will be a mirror image of the pattern that you trace. To have an asymmetrical pattern appear as it does in the book, print a reversed version from the CD. Larger patterns will print on several pages. Trim and tape the pages together as indicated on the pattern to make the full-sized design.

Next, you'll trace the entire pattern on the wrong side of the background fabric. Then, one shape at a time, you'll hold rough-cut appliqué fabrics to the front of the block and baste them from the back along the drawn lines, using a thick needle and thread.

Using the basting stitches as a guide, trim the appliqué fabric to the shape of the motif, leaving a turning allowance.

Clip and remove the basting stitches a few at a time, leaving temporary perforations that serve as stitching guides.

Stitch the motifs from the front as usual, with appliqué needle and thread, and then remove the marks from the back of the finished block. I have provided step-by-step instructions and a practice piece for you on page 42.

Notions

- A large, thick needle (size 7 or 8) for basting
- An appliqué needle; use your favorite. (See the information on page 33.)
- Hand-quilting thread, or any thick thread, in a bright color, for basting
- Appliqué thread; use your favorite. (See the information on page 32.)
- Sharp, pointy hand scissors
- Pins
- Marking implement. I like using a water-erasable marking pen because it's easy to mark with, easy to see, and easily removed. You can also use a marking pencil.
- Light box or light-colored surface

Water-Erasable Caution

If you're using a water-erasable marking pen, test any suspect appliqué fabrics for colorfastness, because it will be necessary to dampen the block to remove the markings. Follow the manufacturer's instructions for removal.

Practice Piece

Here's a full-sized 6" x 6" Heart block for you to practice on. For ease of use, copy or trace this pattern onto a separate sheet of paper, including the centering lines at the edges. Then follow the step-by-step instructions.

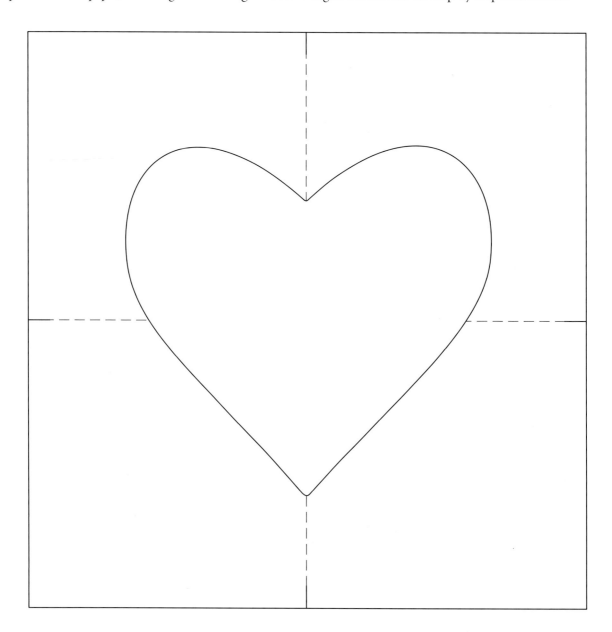

Back-Basting Step-by-Step

At first this method may seem a bit counterintuitive, but follow the steps and back-basting will soon make total sense to you.

1. Cut an oversized (7" x 7") piece of background fabric. (After the block is completed, you'll trim it to the unfinished size.) Fold in quarters and lightly crease the outer edges. Unfold.

2. Place the heart pattern *face up* on a light box or light-colored surface.

3. Place the background fabric *face down* on the pattern. Line up the creases with the centering marks on the pattern.

4. On the back of the fabric, trace the entire pattern. Trace accurately; this is your stitching guide. Do not trace centering lines.

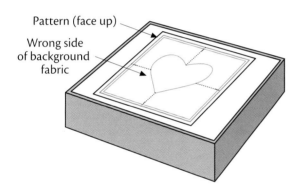

Pattern (face up)

Wrong side of background fabric

5. Rough cut a piece of red fabric that's larger than the heart. Turn the background fabric so the right side faces up and place the red fabric piece, right side up, approximately over the heart tracing.

6. Hold both fabrics up to the light, and viewing from the wrong side of the background, position the red fabric so that it completely covers the marked heart, with at least ¼" margin all the way around. Pin.

Position motif fabric on the front and pin from the back.

7. Thread the basting needle with thick basting thread that contrasts well with the appliqué. With the wrong side of the background facing you, baste through both layers all the way around the heart with a small running stitch exactly on the drawn line. Leave a short tail at the end. Remove the pins.

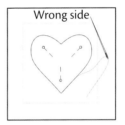
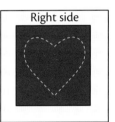

Wrong side

Right side

Baste with small running stitches exactly on drawn line.

Dark Background Fabrics

When using dark fabrics for the background, it may not be possible to see through the fabric to trace the pattern. In this case, you can use tailor's wax-free tracing paper and a tracing wheel or stylus to transfer the pattern to the wrong side of the background fabric. Layer the background fabric wrong side facing up, the tracing paper tracing side down, and the pattern face up. Use the tracing wheel or a stylus to trace the pattern.

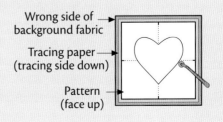

Wrong side of background fabric

Tracing paper (tracing side down)

Pattern (face up)

8. Turn the appliqué over, and from the right side, trim the red fabric to the shape of the heart, about ³⁄₁₆" outside the basting line.

9. Clipping and removing a few basting stitches at a time, tuck the turning allowance under and stitch the heart using an appliqué needle and matching thread.

The appliqué fabric turns easily along the perforations left behind by the basting thread; the perforations in the background fabric serve as a stitching line. Another benefit of this method is that you can also flip the project over now and then to check your stitch positioning against the markings. For information on smooth curves, sharp notches, and pointy points, see "Hand Stitching" on page 45.

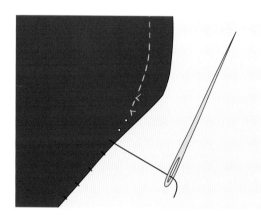

Many patterns have pieces that overlap. Use longer basting stitches on sections of pieces that will be overlapped by another piece, such as the leaf shown. When trimming the appliqué shape on the front, leave a wider margin in the overlapped area.

Front

Once the shape is appliquéd, remove the long basting stitches and either tie off the appliqué thread or use it to baste the overlapped area to the background. (See "Tying Off the Thread" on page 50).

Stems or Vines

There are two reasons I don't use bias strips to make stems or vines with the back-basting method—it's not advisable to iron over the blue water-erasable pen markings, and I don't care for the apples-and-oranges aspect of working both from the back and from the front.

Stems and vines stitch up beautifully with back-basting. Treat them just like any other appliqué shape. They end up just where they're marked without shifting out of place, and the back-basting method helps you stitch them with smooth, even widths.

Now that you have become acquainted with back-basting, use it some more! As with anything new, success and comfort come with practice.

HAND STITCHING

Whether you've used freezer-paper templates or back-basting to prepare your appliqué, now it's time to stitch! From here on in, it's all the same no matter which preparation method you've used. The art shows traditional hand appliqué.

Clipping

In notches, clip almost to the turn line with the tip of your scissors. Fairly steep inside curves will need a series of shallow clips. Do not clip outer curves.

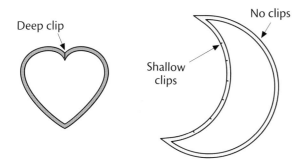

Deep clip

Shallow clips

No clips

Holding the Project

When stitching, hold your work from the bottom in your nonsewing hand. This hand should always stay in a neutral position, without bending or twisting the wrist. Fold or roll the project until you can get an over-and-under grip on the section you're working on, just ahead of where you're stitching. Your thumb is on top and your fingers are underneath. They hold the background and the turned edge of the motif just ahead of where you are placing your stitch.

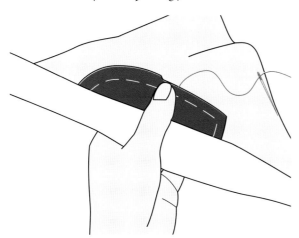

Hold the project from the bottom and keep your wrist relaxed and straight.

Avoid holding the project in any position where your wrist is twisted or bent.

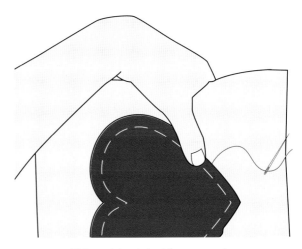

This position is bad for your wrist.

Adjust your grip as often as necessary to get proper access and angle for stitching. Don't let go with your gripping hand. Use your sewing hand to work with the appliqué pieces.

Supporting the Project

Support your work. Holding the project up in midair allows the background fabric to fall away from your hands, which encourages the appliqué to buckle. Put your feet up on a footstool and sew in your lap, not up close to your face. If you need better light or better glasses, gentle quilter, I encourage you to seek ways in which to improve these situations.

The 12" quilter's pressing-and-cutting mat is an excellent appliqué aid. The cushioned side comfortably supports your hand and the project on your lap as you stitch.

Stitching

Load your needle with the fine thread of your choice. Very long lengths of thread will tangle and become worn, so cut yours about 18" to 20" long and put a small, tight knot in the end.

Choose the area where you will begin stitching. Motifs that stand alone can be started anywhere, but it is usually best to start on the straightest part. For circles, you can start anywhere! More about circles later.

If part of the motif is overlapped, begin at the point where it first emerges from the upper motif. Right-handed stitchers sew counterclockwise and left-handers sew clockwise. Fold or roll the project and get a good grip on the selected area with your nonsewing hand (keeping your wrist in a neutral position).

Needle-turn appliqué means just that—the turning allowance is turned under with the needle. I call my personal variation "finger pinch, needle poke." While holding the needle temporarily in my curled-up second finger, I use my forefinger and thumb to tuck and pinch the turning allowance under, less than ½" ahead of where I'm stitching.

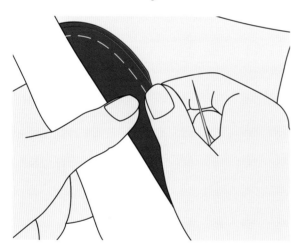

I then use the needle to make small refinements to the stitching edge if needed.

Try using only the needle and try pinching with the finger. Use the technique that you're most comfortable with and that gives you results you like.

To begin, create the first ½" of turned-under edge and hold it with your gripping hand. Some appliquérs bring the needle up inside the fold. I start my thread in the back, bringing my needle up through the background fabric and catching a couple of threads of the fold.

Where do you place your needle tip for the next stitch? You won't really be able to see it, but visualize going back in exactly where you just came out. Avoiding the motif edge, insert the needle tip into the background fabric only, just where the last stitch came out.

Push the needle tip forward just slightly, traveling underneath the background fabric. Come back up through the background a very short distance ahead and catch a couple threads of the fold.

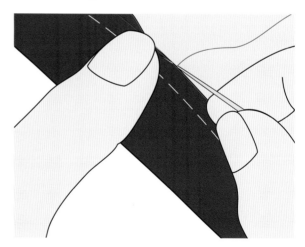

Draw up the thread, pulling it out at a right angle to the edge of the motif. Laying the thread out at a right angle helps you gauge exactly where the last stitch came out. Stitches that are placed ahead or behind this spot will be angled stitches, which are longer and more conspicuous.

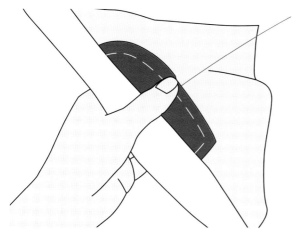

"Sink" your stitches. As you pull up the thread after each stitch, give it a gentle hint of a tug. Not so much as to pull up or pucker the piece, just enough to make it sink into the fold.

Each stitch is taken and pulled up individually. There is no modern shortcut in hand appliqué. Speed increases with experience and confidence. Also, sew with calm hands. Appliqué should not resemble a wrestling match.

Do not turn or sew sections that will be overlapped by another piece.

It's the Tip

However you sew, by hand or machine, appliquéing or piecing, remember that it's what the tip of the needle is doing that's important. The rest of the needle just follows.

Smooth Curves

As you work around a curve, make sure the turning allowance doesn't fold or wrinkle up on itself as you tuck it under. If that happens, you'll get a bump. Don't sew in a bump; it's not going to get better later. Before stitching, take a moment to manipulate the turning allowance underneath the fold with your needle, distributing the bulk and smoothing out the curve.

Points

Stitches are exaggerated for illustration purposes.

1. Sew to within two or three stitches of the point. Trim off the folded-under puppy dog ear that is sticking out on the other side of the point.

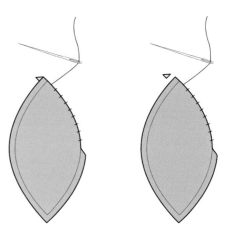

2. Fold the tip under, square across the point.

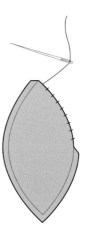

3. Take the remaining stitches to the point, with the last one coming right out of the tip.

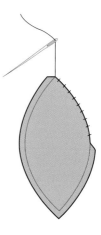

4. Turn the project.

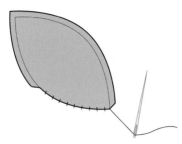

5. Starting at the point, tuck the turning allowance under. Don't try to start ahead and then work back to the point. There will be no room for the turning allowance to go. Work from the point forward.

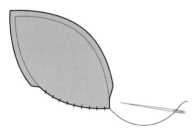

6. When all is arranged satisfactorily and the point looks good, continue to stitch.

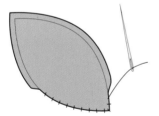

Leaves are a common motif in appliqué, and a great way to practice your points.

Notches

1. Clip the notch almost to the turn line.

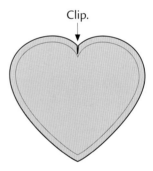

Clip.

2. Sew to within two or three stitches of the notch. There will be very little turning allowance in this area. That's okay. Use very small stitches and tuck under any loose threads.

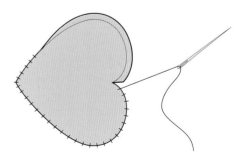

3. Turn the project. Tuck under the first bit of turning allowance on the other side of the notch. In this illustration, some ornery threads from the motif fabric are sticking up in the notch. The needle is not stitching; it is behind the motif, ready to sweep the loose threads under.

4. Use the shaft of the needle to sweep across the notch, creating a tiny fold and encouraging any loose threads to go under. As mentioned before, the needle is still not stitching, just sweeping.

5. Take the remaining stitches to the notch. The last one, directly in the notch, should pick up three or four threads of the motif fabric.

6. Sweep again if necessary. With the tip of the needle, dig under the motif fabric and insert the needle into the background exactly where the last stitch came out. Swing the needle and come out going forward for the next stitch. Snug the thread down well to create a sharp notch.

A heart is a classic motif for learning how to handle both points and notches.

Tying Off the Thread

On the final stitch, insert the needle through the background and pull it all the way through to the back. Turn the block over. Right next to the thread, take a tiny tack in the background fabric beneath the motif and slowly pull the loop down. Before the loop is closed, put the needle through it, and then snug the loop down. (Make another tack if you like, but I decided awhile ago that I would save days and years of my life by only doing one.) Bury the thread tail by running the needle between the background and the motif before cutting off.

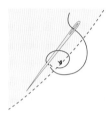

If a raw edge to be left unsewn is of any size, you can run your thread behind the background up into the unsewn margin and baste across it. In this case, I skip the tying off process and finish with a backstitch. The motif isn't going anywhere, because it will be stitched over by another piece.

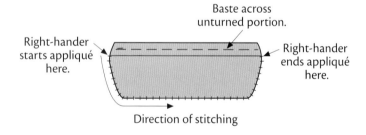

Right-hander starts appliqué here.

Baste across unturned portion.

Right-hander ends appliqué here.

Direction of stitching

Remove the basting and any templates as you complete each piece.

Circles

There are several tools on the market to help make nice circles. Check the gadget section of your favorite quilt shop. A simple low-tech way to make a prepared-edge circle is to use a running stitch to gather the circle around a cardboard or plastic template and then press a crease into it.

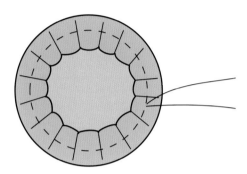

Often, I just appliqué circles like any other shape. If the last little bit of turning allowance is trying to form itself into a bump as it goes under, I use my needle to do some back-and-forth adjustment under the fold to distribute the bulk.

Circles can also be buttons or yo-yos! Consider using these for cute flower centers.

The Final Trim

When all pieces are stitched, press the block. To encourage the appliqué forward instead of mashing it flat, place a fluffy towel on the ironing board, lay the block face down on it, and then press from the back. This is especially important if your blocks are embellished.

After pressing, trim the block to its unfinished size. Now start another, fellow appliqué enthusiast!

Raw-Edge Machine Appliqué

You can show off your thread collection and save some time in the stitching too with this popular appliqué method.

Tools and Notions

- Sewing machine with either a blanket stitch or an adjustable zigzag stitch
- Sharp machine needle in a small size, such as 70/10
- Open-toed presser foot
- Lightweight or regular paper-backed fusible web
- Thread: Just about anything that your sewing machine likes will work, but let's stay away from metallics for right now. You can choose to use either matching or contrasting thread, depending on the look you prefer. A finer thread in a matching or blending color will give a softer, less obvious look. Some machine appliquérs prefer a heavier thread or a contrasting color to give a crisp, well-defined edge. Using black thread and a blanket stitch mimics old-fashioned handwork.
- Fabrics: For raw-edge appliqué, choose fabrics where the color goes all the way through. Avoid fabrics with sketchy or whitish-looking backs. ***Note:*** *The sizing in unwashed fabric may interfere with the bond of the fusible web.*
- Scissors that you don't mind using for cutting paper
- Tracing paper for a placement guide. You may be able to use a light-colored surface or a light box for placement instead, if your background fabric is light.
- Tear-away stabilizer (optional)

Pattern Preparation

With this method, your finished appliqué will be a mirror image of the pattern that you trace. To have an asymmetrical pattern appear as it does in the book, print a *reversed* version from the CD. Larger patterns will print on several pages. Trim and tape the pages together as indicated on the pattern to make the full-sized design. Print an additional *unreversed* pattern for positioning your motifs.

Template Preparation

Each motif needs its own template. Trace each appliqué piece individually on the paper side of the fusible web, leaving at least ½" between pieces. A pencil is fine for this. To denote a portion of a piece that is overlapped by another piece, use a dashed line.

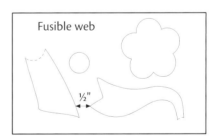

Cut out each template roughly, about ¼" outside the lines.

To reduce stiffness in the finished quilt, remove the center portion of all but the smallest templates. We only need the edge fused anyway, right? Cut right through each template to about ¼" inside the drawn line and cut away the center, leaving a ring of paper-backed fusible web in the shape of the motif.

can also add small pencil marks in the creases at the edges of the right side of the fabric—these will be trimmed away later.)

Positioning Motifs

If your background fabric is light, there's a direct and ingenious way of positioning motifs for machine appliqué. If your pattern is asymmetrical, you've used a reversed version to create the motifs. Now print a regular version to use for positioning. Once you've gotten all your motifs initially fused and cut out, put the regular version of the pattern on the light box or light-colored surface, put the background fabric right side up over it (lined up with centering marks), remove the paper backing from the motifs, and position all of the pieces for the block at once. Carefully transfer to the ironing board for fusing.

For dark backgrounds, you may need to use the overlay method for positioning. You can also use the overlay method for light backgrounds if you like. Trace the entire pattern onto tracing paper. A pencil is fine for this. Also transfer the horizontal and vertical centering lines that are given on each pattern. (Larger sizes of tracing paper are available at stationery or art-supply stores. Or, you can tape together sheets of tracing paper for larger patterns.)

Place the first motif on the background near where you think it might go. Lay the placement guide on top and align the center marks on all four sides with the marks or creases on the background. Without shifting the placement guide, reach underneath and nudge the motif into place. Position all the pieces for the block. When all is satisfactory, carefully transfer to the ironing board for fusing. Or, position everything right on the ironing board, as I do.

Stem or Vines

You can use bias tape for stems or vines (see the information on page 36 for background-fabric preparation and on page 37 for making and placing bias stems). Or you can fuse your stems like any other shape. Wider stems are probably easier to handle by fusing.

Motif Preparation

Using a dry iron and following the manufacturer's recommendations, press the templates fusible side down onto the *wrong* side of the appliqué fabrics.

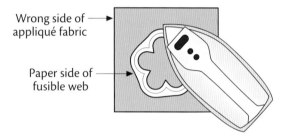

Wrong side of appliqué fabric

Paper side of fusible web

Allow fabric and templates to cool briefly. Handling as little as possible, cut the motif area apart from the main body of the fabric, and then roughly cut the motifs apart.

The next step is to carefully cut out the motifs exactly on the drawn lines. However, you'll need to leave a little margin on any portion that will be overlapped by another piece, as indicated by a dashed line on the template.

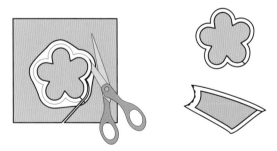

Background-Fabric Preparation

Cut the background square a little larger than the unfinished size. For an 8" block (8½" unfinished), cut the background at least 9" square. After the block is completed, you'll trim it to the unfinished size.

To create positioning marks, fold the background square in quarters and crease the outer edges. (You

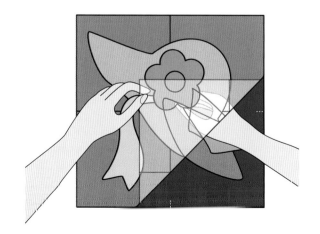

Fusing

Following the manufacturer's recommendations, steam press the appliqué pieces until they are bonded to the background. Don't move the iron back and forth across the motifs; just pick up the iron and set it down until all sections are fused. Let cool, and then move to the sewing machine.

Sewing

Start by testing your stitching on a scrap project. Using a blanket stitch or a narrow zigzag stitch and the thread of your choice, experiment with stitch length and width until you are satisfied with the tension and the appearance of the stitching.

For blanket stitching, the length of the forward stitch and the sideways stitch should be the same. The forward stitches go into the background fabric, right next to the motif. The sideways stitches go into the motif at a right angle to the edge.

If you have any trouble with "tunneling" (stitching that puckers the project), use tearaway stabilizer underneath your project and remove it once you're finished sewing.

Sew slowly and steer around curves as much as you can. Stop with the needle down in the background fabric whenever you need to pivot. Make slight pivots more often around steeper curves. Remember, the goal is to keep the sideways stitches biting into the appliqué at a right angle to the edge.

I'm fond of matching the thread to the motif. If you do this too, sew all the pink, then all the red, and so on, before changing threads.

To be very neat, draw the bobbin thread up to the top when beginning and ending your line of stitching. Then thread both threads onto a large-eyed needle and pull them through to the back, burying them before cutting off.

That's machine appliqué—another one for your appliqué bag of tricks!

A Little Gallery of Ideas

Some of the blocks in this collection recall traditional appliqué motifs, while others are modern, fun, or whimsical in nature. Choose your favorites and put them together or sprinkle a few into your next project. Make one block or many. Make them large or small. Mix and match them. The quilts you make will celebrate your own style and personality.

Put some blocks in a big sampler quilt or make a cute table runner. Sometimes you just need one block to contribute to an exchange or as a thank-you for a guild officer—these designs are a great resource. A block that speaks to you could be a banner hanging in a special place in your home. Stitch up a wall quilt using designs that you like and your favorite appliqué method. What could be more fun than that? Decorate an apron or a tote bag. The possibilities are endless!

Here are some examples for your inspiration. The Martingale & Company staff members and I had so much fun creating these simple wall quilts, both on the computer and in the fabric. We've provided information about the block sizes, sashing, and border dimensions in case you'd like to make something similar.

Enjoy the blocks!

There's One in Every Crowd

by Kay Mackenzie. A Westie is crashing the Scottie party! The same block repeated with a little change or twist somewhere creates a nice surprise. This quilt was machine appliquéd and machine quilted. I used buttons for the license tags.

    Block size: 6" x 6"
    Sashing width: ¾"
    Sashing cornerstones: ¾" x ¾"
    Border width: 2"
    Finished size: 17" x 24"

The Mackenzie Family Quilt

by Kay Mackenzie. Each of the blocks in this funny little wall quilt has special meaning for me and my husband, Dana. The pi symbol (π) is for him; he is a mathematician and used to teach at Duke University, which is why it's "Duke blue." This quilt was hand appliquéd using freezer-paper templates and then hand quilted.

> Block size: 6" x 6"
> Sashing width ½"
> Sashing cornerstones: ½" x ½"
> Border width: 2½"
> Border corners: 2½" x 2½"
> Finished size: 25" x 25"

Finding Pi. If you have a mathematician in mind and would also like to appliqué a pi, choose a typeface that has a good-looking pi symbol and print it out in a very large size to use for your pattern. The pi symbol may be found under "Special Characters" or "Symbols" in most text-editing programs. If there is no pi in your current character set, try another typeface.

Blooms in Red and Yellow

by Kay Mackenzie. Arrange some of the floral designs using your favorite colors for a beautiful bouquet sampler. This quilt was hand appliquéd using back-basting and then machine quilted.

Block size: 8" x 8"
End blocks, middle row: 3½" x 8"
Sashing width: 1"
Border width: 2"
Finished size: 32" x 32"

Pie and Coffee. This would go great in the kitchen!

    Coffee Mug block size: 6" x 6", with two 1"-wide strips added to top and bottom

    Cherry Pie block size: 10" x 10"

    Coffeepot block size: 8" x 8", with two 1"-wide strips added to top and bottom

    Border width: 2"

    Border cornerstones: 2" x 2"

    Finished quilt size: 28" x 14"

Birds and Blossoms designed by Adrienne Smitke.

Say hello to spring with this cheerful table runner (below).

    Bird House block size: 12" x 12"

    Bird on Branch block size: 6" x 6"

    Wreath block size: 6" x 6"

    Heart and Buds block size: 6" x 6"

    Cardinal block size: 6" x 6"

    Sashing strip width: 1½"

    Border width: 2"

    Border cornerstones: 2" x 2"

    Finished quilt size: 19" x 34"

Welcome Banner. The pineapple as a symbol of
hospitality could hang in your entryway, welcoming
you and your visitors to your home.

Welcome block size: 10" x 10"
Top and bottom strip width: 1"
Alternating rectangles: 2" x 3"
Finished size: 10" x 18"

Cat and Mouse designed by Robin Strobel. The mice come out to play while the cat dreams away. Try experimenting with fun novelty prints for the cat.

Cat Dream block size: 9" x 9"
Mouse block cornerstones: 3" x 3". (The Mouse blocks on the lower right and upper left are reversed.)
Border width: 3"
Finished size: 15" x 15"

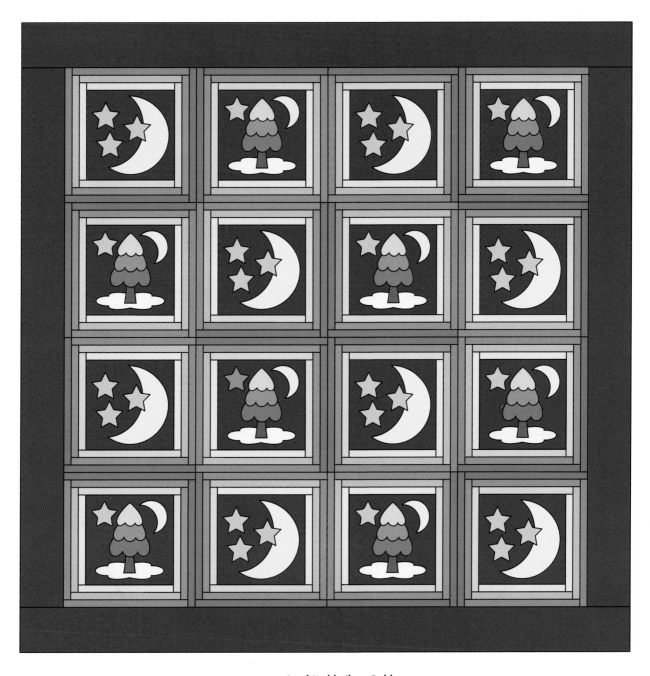

Good Night, Sleep Tight designed by Robin Strobel. Nestle your favorite blocks in a Log Cabin frame or inside a Star block. Many of the appliqué blocks have a definite "up" and "down," so take care to add the Log Cabin strips to the correct sides. The Moon and Stars blocks and Tree blocks are 6" x 6" centers for ½"-wide finished Log Cabin strips.

Finished block size: 9" x 9"
Border width: 3"
Finished size: 42" x 42"

ABOUT THE AUTHOR

gregory case photography

Lacking any sort of quilting heritage, Kay started without a stitch of knowledge in a beginning quilting class, circa 1992. When Kay told her instructor that she enjoyed the Dresden Plate the most out of all the blocks in the sampler, the instructor said, "You just might be an appliqué person." Kay wonders to this day whether that observation shaped her destiny, because it turned out to be so true!

From that class on, Kay was gripped with the quilt pox, happily and at all times working on a project—or eight! Over the years she developed the yen to create her own designs to appliqué. When she took some digital-media classes and learned computer illustration, designing appliqué became a reality for her.

Kay considers herself a quilter who writes—or a writer who quilts. Either way you look at it, she lives in Santa Cruz, California, with her husband, Dana Mackenzie, who is a science journalist. Their family consists of three cats and their little papillon, Willie.

Kay blogs about appliqué at www.allaboutapplique.net. Also visit her website at www.quiltpuppy.com. And, when you make something using her designs, be sure to submit it for "Show and Tell" at www.kaymackenzie.com.

New and Best-Selling Titles from

 **That Patchwork Place®** America's Best-Loved Quilt Books®

 **Martingale® & COMPANY**

America's Best-Loved Craft & Hobby Books®
America's Best-Loved Knitting Books®

APPLIQUÉ
Applique Quilt Revival
Beautiful Blooms
Cutting-Garden Quilts
Dream Landscapes—*NEW!*
More Fabulous Flowers
Sunbonnet Sue and Scottie Too

BABIES AND CHILDREN
Baby's First Quilts—*NEW!*
Baby Wraps
Even More Quilts for Baby
Let's Pretend—*NEW!*
The Little Box of Baby Quilts
Snuggle-and-Learn Quilts for Kids
Sweet and Simple Baby Quilts

BEGINNER
Color for the Terrified Quilter
Happy Endings, Revised Edition
Machine Appliqué for the Terrified Quilter
Your First Quilt Book (or it should be!)

GENERAL QUILTMAKING
Adventures in Circles
American Jane's Quilts for All Seasons—*NEW!*
Bits and Pieces
Charmed
Cool Girls Quilt
Country-Fresh Quilts—*NEW!*
Creating Your Perfect Quilting Space
Follow-the-Line Quilting Designs Volume Three
Gathered from the Garden
The New Handmade—*NEW!*
Points of View
Positively Postcards
Prairie Children and Their Quilts
Quilt Revival
A Quilter's Diary
Quilter's Happy Hour
Quilting for Joy—*NEW!*
Sensational Sashiko
Simple Seasons
Skinny Quilts and Table Runners

Twice Quilted
Young at Heart Quilts

HOLIDAY AND SEASONAL
Christmas Quilts from Hopscotch
Christmas with Artful Offerings
Comfort and Joy
Holiday Wrappings

HOOKED RUGS, NEEDLE FELTING, AND PUNCHNEEDLE
The Americana Collection
Miniature Punchneedle Embroidery
Needle-Felting Magic
Needle Felting with Cotton and Wool
Punchneedle Fun

PAPER PIECING
Easy Reversible Vests, Revised Edition—*NEW!*
Paper-Pieced Mini Quilts
Show Me How to Paper Piece
Showstopping Quilts to Foundation Piece
A Year of Paper Piecing

PIECING
501 Rotary-Cut Quilt Blocks—*NEW!*
Better by the Dozen
Favorite Traditional Quilts Made Easy—*NEW!*
Loose Change—*NEW!*
Maple Leaf Quilts
Mosaic Picture Quilts
New Cuts for New Quilts
Nine by Nine
On-Point Quilts
Quiltastic Curves
Ribbon Star Quilts
Rolling Along
Sew One and You're Done

QUICK QUILTS
40 Fabulous Quick-Cut Quilts
Instant Bargello
Quilts on the Double
Sew Fun, Sew Colorful Quilts

SCRAP QUILTS
Nickel Quilts
Save the Scraps
Simple Strategies for Scrap Quilts
Spotlight on Scraps

CRAFTS
Art from the Heart
The Beader's Handbook
Card Design
Crochet for Beaders
Dolly Mama Beads
Embellished Memories—*NEW!*
Friendship Bracelets All Grown Up
Making Beautiful Jewelry—*NEW!*
Paper It!—*NEW!*
Sculpted Threads
Sew Sentimental
Trading Card Treasures—*NEW!*

KNITTING & CROCHET
365 Crochet Stitches a Year
365 Knitting Stitches a Year
A to Z of Knitting
All about Knitting—*NEW!*
Amigurumi World
Beyond Wool—*NEW!*
Cable Confidence
Casual, Elegant Knits
Chic Knits
Crocheted Pursenalities
Gigi Knits…and Purls
Kitty Knits
Knitted Finger Puppets—*NEW!*
The Knitter's Book of Finishing Techniques
Knitting Circles around Socks
Knitting with Gigi
More Sensational Knitted Socks
Pursenalities
Skein for Skein
Toe-Up Techniques for Hand Knit Socks, Revised Edition—*NEW!*
Together or Separate—*NEW!*

Our books are available at bookstores and your favorite craft, fabric, and yarn retailers. If you don't see the title you're looking for, visit us at **www.martingale-pub.com** or contact us at:

1-800-426-3126

International: 1-425-483-3313
Fax: 1-425-486-7596 • Email: info@martingale-pub.com

9/08